NEWCAS

Wit & Humour

TIM E RIVER

BRADWELL
BOOKS

Published by Bradwell Books
9 Orgreave Close Sheffield S13 9NP
Email: books@bradwellbooks.co.uk
Compiled by Tim E River

British Library Cataloguing in Publication Data: a catalogue record for
this book is available from the British Library.

1st Edition

ISBN: 9781909914452

Print: Gomer Press, Llandysul, Ceredigion SA44 4JL
Design by: jenksdesign@yahoo.co.uk/07506 471162
Illustrations: ©Tim O'Brien 2014

The Newcastle temperature scale

50ºF - Southerners turn on their heating. People in Newcastle do their gardening.

40ºF - Southerners shiver uncontrollably. People in Newcastle sunbathe.

35ºF - Southerners' cars won't start. People in Newcastle drive with the windows down.

15ºF - Southerners begin to evacuate. People in Newcastle go swimming in the North Sea.

0ºF - Southern landlords turn up the heat. People in Newcastle have their final barbecue before it starts to get cold.

-10ºF - Southerners are freezing. People in Newcastle throw on a light jacket.

-80ºF - Polar bears wonder if it's worth it. Boy scouts in Newcastle wear long trousers.

-100ºF - Santa Claus abandons the North Pole. People in Newcastle put on their long johns

-173ºF - Alcohol freezes. People in Newcastle become frustrated because the pubs are shut.

-297ºF - Microbial life starts to disappear. The cows on Newcastle Town Moor complain of vets with cold hands

-460ºF - All atomic motion stops. People in Newcastle start to stamp their feet and blow on their hands.

-500ºF - Hell freezes over. Sunderland qualify for Europe.

What do Newcastle, Middlesbrough and Sunderland have in common?

Newcastle: Woodgate

Middlesbrough: Southgate

Sunderland: Relegate

A visitor from outside the area was driving around Parklands in his fancy new car and found that he was lost. The driver stopped old Tom and said, "You there! Old man, what happens if I turn left here?"

"Don't know sir," replied old Tom.

"Well, what if I turn right here, where will that take me?" continued the visitor. "Don't know, sir." replied old Tom. Becoming exasperated, the driver continued, "Well, what if I go straight on?" A flicker of knowledge moved over old Tom's face until he replied, "Don't know, sir."

"I say old man you don't know a lot, do you?" retorted the posh bloke. Old Tom looked at him and said, "I may not know a lot, but I ain't lost like you are!" With that, old Tom walked off leaving the motorist stranded.

Two Mackems were walking around Newcastle when they stopped at a shop and looked in the window. One Mackem said to the other, "Look! Shirts £1, quilts £1.50, sheets, 50p. It's so cheap here, I'm going to buy loads and sell them back home." So he walked in and asked to buy 20 shirts, quilts and sheets. The woman at the counter said "You're a Mackem, aren't you?" to which he replied "How did you know?" The woman answered "This is a dry cleaner's."

A Mackem walked into a Geordie pub and said "Who wants to hear a joke about Newcastle United?" A big bloke got up and said: "Listen man, I'm 6 foot 3, weighing in at 90 kilos." Then he pointed at the man in the Newcastle shirt to his left. "And my friend here is 6 foot 6 and weighs more than 100 kilos." Pointing to another tall man in full Newcastle United outfit, he added: "That bloke over there is a former youth boxing champion. See, you're outnumbered, 3 against 1. So, do you still want to tell your joke?" The Mackem answered: "Well, no. Because I don't like to explain the same joke three times…"

A Consultant Heart Surgeon at the local hospital arrived at a Geordie man's bed and pulled back the curtain

"How are you doing Mr Jones?" he asked the man

"Wey not too bad Doctor ye knaa, cannit grumble"

"Well I suppose you could, Mr Smith. I've been looking at your latest test results and you have a huge amount of damage to the arteries supplying blood to your heart. Can I ask if you smoke?"

"Wey ah have a couple a day ye knaa, nee more than 2 packets of backy a week though"

"I see, and how long have you been smoking?", asked the consultant

"Wey about 60 years now like", replied Geordie

"So you started when you were were about one then?" replied the consultant drily

"Nah Man Doctor, ye cheeky get! … I was at least ten or eleven like"

A man went to see a Geordie doctor and said "Doctor! Me armpits smell of coconuts!" The doctor replied "Well, they're bounty."

A Geordie had a big lottery win so he decided to go on a world cruise with his best mate, Tim. After a week at sea, the Captain called the Purser into his cabin to ask which influential people were on board, so he could invite them to his table.

"Sir", said the Purser, "We have four film stars, three M.P.'s and two strange gentlemen from the North, who seem to be very wealthy."

The Captain instructed him to go round with invitations. Knocking on the Geordie's cabin door, he was told to come in. When he entered; there were the two Geordies with four bottles of brown ale, eating fish and chips.

The Purser saluted, "Begging your pardon, gentlemen", he said,

"The Captain's compliments. He requests your company at his table tonight."

"Ye must be joking", says the first Geordie,

"Ye divvent think Tim and me's gan te spend aal this money to eat with the crew."

What is the difference between a Kangaroo and a Kangaroot

A Kangaroo is a Marsupial native to Australia

A Kangaroot is what a Geordie says if he's stuck in a lift.

One night a Geordie man was having a pint in his local when he saw a man wearing a very unusual pair of shoes! The Geordie man couldn't keep his eyes off them so he said to the man.

"How mistor! Whatha kind ov shoes is them ye hev on? I'd like to hev a pair of them."

"Why!" said the man, "They are Crocodile Shoes."

"Why lad!" said the Geordie "I must be thick in the heed but what's a Crocodile?"

"Well!" replied the other man, "A crocodile is a reptile, which inhabits the rivers of Africa. The River Zambesi is full of them."

"Thanks mistor!" said the Geordie, "I'll hev te hev a pair of them shoes."

So the Geordie saved two weeks' pay and booked a plane to Africa. Paddling his canoe up the Zambesi, he saw a huge Crocodile. The man jumped off the boat, swam towards the beast, fought it, killed it, dragged it ashore, looked at it and said,

"By heck! Eftor all that trouble, it's got ne shoes on!"

How many Sunderland fans does it take to change a light bulb?

None, they're all happy living in Newcastle's shadow!

A rather cocky man working on a busy construction site in Chinatown was bragging that he could outdo anyone in a feat of strength. He made a special case of making fun of Morris, one of the more senior workmen. After several minutes, Morris had had enough.

"Why don't you put your money where your mouth is?" he said. "I'll bet a week's wages that I can haul something in a wheelbarrow over to that outbuilding that you won't be able to wheel back."

"You're on, mate," the over confident young man replied. "It's a bet! Let's see what you got."

Morris reached out and grabbed the wheelbarrow by the handles. Then, nodding to the young man, he said, "All right. Get in."

One day, Cheryl Cole went to the hairdressers in Newcastle.

"Alreet, bonnie lass. What d'yee fancy the day, like?"

"I think I'd like a perm" "Certainly. Mary haird a little lairm."

A Geordie man said to his friend "The wife's having a bairn in hospital today! She's gone into labour!" His friend asked: "What stage is she is at? Is she dilated?" "Wey man" said Geordie "We're both of us over the moon!"

At a pub in Heaton, a special act was put on to entertain the regulars: a magician. He was a traditional style magician so he was pulling coins out of ears, matches out of matchboxes and so in. At the end of his act, he said to one elderly regular, "Did you enjoy my act then?" "By hinney! Aa did an aal" said the Geordie man. The magician replied "Would you be surprised if I put my hand in your jacket pocket and pulled a rabbit out?" "I waald, an aal" said the regular. "I've got a ferret in there!"

One day a Southerner said to his friend from Newcastle "Do you know any card games?" His friend replied "Aye ice hockey."

"That's not a card game!" said the Southerner. The Geordie replied "It's the cardest game ah knar."

A Geordie came home after a long day at work. His wife had a leek pudding waiting on the table for him. The Geordie looked at it. "That's a big leek pudding it'll be for wor Jim."

"No", said his wife. "It's not for wor Jimmy."

"But it's the biggest leek pudding I've seen" replied the man. "A na then it's for wor Tommy."

"No" she said, "It's not for wor Tommy."

"Mind it's a monster." said the man. "I bet it's for wor Willie." "You're wrang," she replied again "It's not for your Willie."

"Why lass whe's it for?" asked the Geordie "Cos it's sartinly a big u."

"Why" said his wife "If ye must knaa it's for ye."

"Blimey." said the Geordie. "What a little un."

Did you hear about the lorry driver from Woolsington who was seen desperately chiselling away at the brickwork after his lorry got stuck while passing through a tunnel?

"Why don't you let some air out of your tyres?" asked a helpful passer-by.

"Nah, man," replied the driver "It's the roof that won't go under, not the wheels."

One day a Geordie was out and about when he saw a grand funeral procession making its way up the road. There was a brass band, plumed horses pulling the hearse, six coaches and hundreds of mourners in silk hats walking behind it! The Geordie thought to himself "He must be an important bloke. That must be a Lord Mayor or Chief of Police or something. I'll just ax this young lad, he might know who he is". "Mate," said Geordie. "D'ye knaa whe it is that's deed ower thonder." "Eee I'm not sure," said the paper boy, "But I think it's that bloke in the forst carriage."

Two Geordie donkeys were in a rowing boat. One said "Eeyore," the other replied "Cheeky one! Ye Oar!"

A Geordie once bought a talking budgie. To his disappointment, all it wanted to say was "I'm a Geordie budgie and I'm hard as nails" The budgie repeated the same words over and over for a few weeks until the man eventually grew sick and tired of the budgie. So he bought a hawk. He put the hawk in the cage with the budgie before going to bed and said "Let's see how hard you are now, you little git" and went off to bed.

In the morning he checked the cage. The hawk was dead and the budgie was hopping about shouting "I'm a Geordie budgie and I'm hard as nails." It continued to repeat this all day so the next day the man went and got a buzzard. "Right then this fella will sort you out for sure." said the man as he put it in the cage. Off he went

When he returned, he was amazed to find the buzzard dead and the budgie happliy shouting "I'm a Geordie budgie and I'm hard as nails" The man made a few calls and got hold of an eagle.

He put the eagle into the cage before going to bed. He told the budgie There is no way you're still going to be here in the morning, mate." And went off to bed.

In the morning he came down to find the eagle dead, but the budgie completely without feathers. Amazed, he stared at the budgie who still looking happy said "I'm a Geordie budgie and I'm hard as nails, but I had to take my coat off for that one."

A Geordie scout worked for General Custer just before the events of Little Big Horn took place. One day Custer said "Git on that thar hoss and ride over them thar hills and see if you can find any Indians."

"All reet sor, am on me way." replied the Geordie. Two days later the Geordie rode back into the fort with arrows in his hat and arrows in his saddle saying "Sor, Sor, Just ower them hills is thoosands and thoosands of Indians."

"What are they a doing?" said Custer
"Wey they'r playin drums." said Geordie.

"Are they war drums?" asked Custer
"Wey no man, Aa think they're theors."

A man walked up to the foreman of a road laying gang in Jesmond and asked for a job. "I haven't got one for you today." said the foreman looking up from his newspaper. "But if you walk half a mile down here, you can see if you like the work and I can put you on the list for tomorrow." "That's great, mate," said the bloke as he wandered off down the road to find the gang. At the end of the shift, the man walked past the foreman and shouted, "Thanks mate. See you tomorrow." The foreman looked up from his paper and shouted back, "You've enjoyed yourself then?". "Yes, I have!" shouted back the bloke, "But can I have a shovel or a pick to lean on like the rest of the gang?"

Back in Viking days a Geordie man used to stand on the edge of the coast to look out for raiders. One night he heard a splash of oars so he called out

"Whe's theor" and from the fog a Nordic voice replied "Anna" (The name of the longship)

The Geordie man thought for a moment then shouted back

"A Kna ye kna, but I diven't kna cos a cannit see yer thru this fog!"

A Geordie man went to sign on at the job centre. The man there said "I've got just the job for you. Can you drive?"

"I can anaal." said the Geordie.

"Well," said the job centre assistant "you can start tomorrow as a driver/conductor on a city centre bus. That means you drive as well as collecting fares."

So the next day, the Geordie got on the road with his double-decker bus. At about three in the afternoon the phone rang in the bus depot. The Geordie was on the phone, "Can ye git oot here sharp? The bus has gone through a shop window, broken glass aall ower."

"Oh no!" said the inspector on the other end, "How did it happen?

"I divvent knaa," said the Geordie "I was upstairs taking the fares at the time!"

A Geordie boy was writing about his holidays on his first day back at school and penned, "Me and me dad, us went fishing."

The teacher looked over his shoulder and said, "We went fishing!"

"Why," exclaimed the lad in a puzzled tone, "Me and me dad."

A little Geordie boy came home from school, crying, "Ma!" he said, "Aal me mates at school keep caalin me big heed, hevn't ah not got a big heed Ma?" "Of course ye haven't got a big heed son," said his mother. "Just nip doon te the corner shop and get me three stone of taties.........in yor cap!"

A Geordie went to the optician's. The optician said "Can you see that board?

The Geordie replied "Bord!? I can't even see a cage!"

A man from Sunderland and a man from Newcastle from ended up sitting next to each other on a flight to airport. The Mackem started thinking that he could have some fun at the Geordie's expense and asked him if he'd like to play a fun game. The Geordie man was tired and just wanted to relax. He politely declined the offer and tried to sleep. The Mackem persisted, explaining:

"I ask you a question, and if you don't know the answer, you pay me only £5; you ask me one, and if I don't know the answer, I will pay you £500."

This got the Geordie a little more interested and he finally agreed to play the game.

The Mackem asked the first question,"What's the distance from the Earth to the moon?"

The Geordie said nothing, but reached into his pocket, pulled out a five-pound note and handed it to the Mackem.

Now, it was the Geordie's turn. He asked the Mackem, "What goes up a hill with three legs, and comes down with four?"

The Mackem used his laptop. He used the air-phone; he searched the web, he sent emails to his most well read friends, but still came up with nothing. After over an hour of searching, he finally gave up.

He woke the Geordie up and handed him £500. The man smugly pocketed the cash and went straight back to sleep.

The Mackem went wild with curiosity wanting to hear the answer. He woke the businessman up and asked, "Well? What goes up a hill with three legs and comes down with four?"

The Geordie reached into his pocket, handed the Mackem £5 and went back to sleep.

A Geordie was driving home from work when his car broke down. He got out of the car to find smoke pouring out of his bonnet. He quickly got on his mobile to contact his local garage "Hello mate, me cars broken doon and I divvent knar whats gannin on but there's smoke coming from me bonnet."

The mechanic on the other end of the phone replied "Are you owa heatin'?"

The man said "Nah, I'm just on the Byker Bridge."

What is the difference between a battery and a Mackem? A battery has a positive side.

At the local derby, a big group of Sunderland supporters, unable to get tickets, stood outside the stadium shouting up at Newcastle United supporters for updates on the state of play. Suddenly there was a massive roar from the crowd, so Mackems outside shouted up, "What's happening? What's happening?" The Newcastle supporters shouted back, "All the Sunderland team have been carried off injured. There's only one player left on the field." Ten minutes passed. Then there was another massive roar from the crowd. The Mackems shouted up "What's happening? Our player scored, has he?"

Robert proudly drove his new convertible into Newcastle with an unwanted gift, a footspa, on the back seat.

He had walked half way around the block from the parked car when he realised that he had left the top down... with the footspa on the back seat.

He ran all the way back to his car, but it was too late... Another five footspas had been dumped in the car.

Three Newcastle United fans and three Sunderland fans were going on day trip by train. At the train station, the three Mackems each bought their tickets and watched in confusion as the three Geordies bought just one ticket between them. "How are three people going to travel on only one ticket?" asked one of the Sunderland group. "Watch this!" answered one of the Geordies.

The group got onto the train. But while the Sunderland fans sat in their seats, all three of the Geordies crowded into the train toilet and closed the door behind them.

Shortly after the train left, the conductor came round to check tickets. He knocked on the toilet door and said, "Ticket, please!" The door opened a fraction and a single arm emerged with a ticket in hand. The conductor took it, checked it and moved on.

The Sunderland fans watched all this and agreed it was quite a clever idea. So, on the return trip, they decided to copy the Newcastle fans on the return trip and save some money. When they got to the station, they bought a single ticket for the return trip. To their astonishment, the Geordies didn't buy a ticket at all. "How are you going to travel without a ticket?" asked one perplexed Sunderland follower. "Watch" said one of the Geordies.

When they got onto the train the three Sunderland fans all crammed together into a toilet and the three Mackems squished into another one nearby. The train started up. Shortly afterwards, one of the Geordies left the toilet and walked over to the toilet in which the Sunderland fans were hiding. He knocked on the door and said, "Ticket, please."

A man went to the doctor one day and said: "I've just been playing football for Sunderland and when I got back, I found that when I touched my legs, my arms, my head and everywhere else, it really hurt."

After a careful examination the doctor said: "You've broken your finger."

The Seven Dwarves were walking through the forest one day when they suddenly fell into a deep ravine. Snow White, who was following along behind her friends, stared over the edge of the ravine and called out to the dwarfs. From the very depths of the dark hole a voice came back, "Sunderland are dead certs for the Premiership."

Snow White heaved a sigh of relief, thinking "Well, at least Dopey's survived!"

Why were Sunderland late for their next big match? They were stuck on a broken escalator!

Supporters waiting to watch Newcastle play Sunderland heard that the Sunderland players were going to be delayed.

The team had passed a sign on the way saying 'Clean Lavatories'...so they did.

A priest was having a well deserved day off in Whitley Bay when he saw two Newcastle supporters out in a boat. Suddenly he noticed that in the water, a Sunderland fan was being attacked by a shark. Fortunately, a boat arrived and the Newcastle fans pulled the Mackem into the boat to safety, killed the shark and pulled it onto the boat.

The priest beckoned the boat to the shore and said "I've never seen anything so brave. I understood that there was intense rivalry between Newcastle fans and Sunderland fans, but that has restored my faith in mankind". He then blessed the men and left.

One of the locals turned to his friend and asked "What was he on about?" "Dunno" said his mate "But he knows nothing about shark fishing. Do we need any fresh bait?"

When Steve moved to London he constantly annoyed his new acquaintances by boasting about how great his home town of Newcastle was.

Finally, in exasperation, one said, "If Newcastle is so wonderful, how come you didn't stay there?" "Well," answered Steve "They're all so clever up there I had to come down here to have any chance of making it at all."

They say that a man from Sunderland laughs three times at a joke: the first time when everybody gets it, the second a week later when he thinks he gets it, the third time a month later when somebody explains it to him.

At a well established manufacturing business in Newcastle, the young boss had the sad responsibility of telling one of the workers, Joe, that it was time for him to retire after 60 years with the company.

The old man was outraged:

"So, it's come to this, has it? I'm not wanted any longer?" he protested.

"I worked for your father, your grandfather and his dad too. I tell you what, young man, if I'd known that this job wasn't going to be permanent, I would never have taken it on."

A passenger in a taxi travelling through Ouseburn tapped the driver on the shoulder to ask him something. The driver screamed, lost control of the cab, nearly hit a bus, drove up over the curb and stopped just inches from a large plate glass window.

For a few moments everything was silent in the cab, then the driver said, "Please, don't ever do that again. You scared the daylights out of me."

The passenger, who was also frightened, apologised and said he didn't realise that a tap on the shoulder could frighten him so much, to which the driver replied, "I'm sorry, it's really not your fault at all. Today is my first day driving a cab. I've been driving a hearse for the last 25 years."

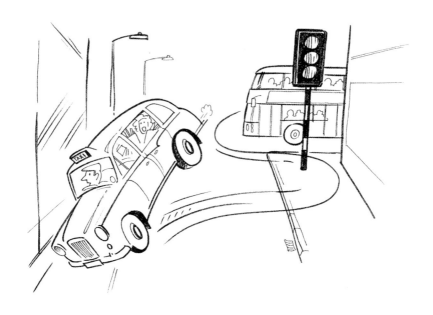

One day a Newcastle fan arrived at St James Park for a big match. He was running a bit late and the match soon kicked off. The fan was surprised to notice that the seat next to him was still empty. He asked the man on the other side of the empty seat if the person was with him.

"No." answered the man, "It's my wife's seat, but she died suddenly."

"Oh I'm so sorry, mate," said the other man "...couldn't you have given it to a friend or relative or something?

"I would have done" said the other man, "But they've all gone to the funeral."

Two blokes from Benton went into a pub.

The first man said "A pint o' bitter, and a half o' shandy for my mate 'Donkey', please!"

The publican replied "What's with him calling you 'Donkey'?"

The second one said "Oh, 'e aw, 'e aw, 'e always calls me that!"

How many Mackems does it take to change a light bulb? Two - one to change the bulb, the other to say loudly how he did it as well as any Newcastle fan.

A man from Kingston Park was staggering home one evening, after a heavy night at the pub with his friends.

He suddenly noticed a man from the water board with a big 'T' handle, in the middle of the road opening a valve at the bottom of a manhole.

He walked up behind him and gave him a shove.

"What was that for?" asked the startled man.

The drunken man replied, "That's for turning all the streets round when I'm trying to find my way home!"

Have you heard about the latest machine on the pier at Whitley Bay?

You put ten pence in and ask it any question and it gives you a true answer.

One holiday maker from Sunderland tried it last week.

He asked the machine "Where is my father?" The machine replied:

"Your father is fishing in Berwick."

Well, he thought, that's daft for a start because my father is dead.

"Where is my mother's husband?"

Back came the reply, "Your mother's husband is buried in Sunderland, but your father is still fishing in Berwick."

A Blakelaw man fell out with his in-laws and banned them from entering the house while he was in it. His wife faithfully carried out his wishes until she was on her death bed and then asked sadly, "Haven't I always been a supportive wife to you, John?" "Yes my dear." He replied "The best"." Then I would love it if you could grant my last request and let my sister Sarah ride in the first car with you at my funeral?" "Alright, my dear" he agreed heavily, "But I'm warning you, it'll spoil all my pleasure!"

It was a quiet night in Fawdon and a man and his wife were tucked up in bed fast asleep when there was an unexpected knock on the door. The man looked at his clock and saw that it was half past three in the morning. "I'm not getting out of bed at this time of the night," he thought, and rolled over.

A louder knock followed. "Aren't you going to answer that?" asked his wife sleepily.

So the man dragged himself out of bed and went downstairs. He opened the door and saw that there was a strange man standing at the door. It didn't take the homeowner long to realise that the man was drunk.

"Hi there," slurred the stranger. "Can you give me a push?"

"No, I'm sorry. It's half past three. I was in bed," said the man and slammed the door. He went back up to bed and told his wife what happened.

"That wasn't very nice of you," she said

"Remember that night we broke down in the pouring rain on the way to pick the kids up from the babysitter, and you had to knock on that man's door to get us started again? What would have happened if he'd told us to get lost?"

"But the man who just knocked on our door was drunk," replied her husband.

"Well we can at least help move his car somewhere safe and sort him out a taxi," said his wife. "He needs our help." So the husband got out of bed again, got dressed, and went downstairs. He opened the door, but couldn't to see the stranger anywhere so he shouted, "Hey, do you still want a push?" In answer, he heard a voice call out, "Yes please!" So, still being unable to see the stranger, he shouted, "Where are you?"

"I'm over here," the stranger replied, "on your swing."

Pete and Larry hadn't seen each other in many years. They were having a long chat, telling each other all about their lives. Finally Pete invited Larry to visit him in his new apartment in Newcastle city centre. "I have a wife and three kids and I'd love to have you visit us."

"Great. Where do you live?

"Here's the address. There's plenty of parking behind the flat. Park and come around to the front door, kick it open with your foot, go to the lift and press the button with your left elbow, then enter! When you reach the sixth floor, go down the hall until you see my name on the door. Then press the doorbell with your right elbow and I'll let you in."

"Great. But tell me...what is all this business of kicking the front door open, then pressing lift buttons with my right, then my left elbow?"

Pete answered, "Surely you're not coming empty-handed?"

A father and his son, Bobby, arrived at the big match at St James' Park and Dad suddenly realised that he couldn't find their tickets. He said to his son, "Nip home and see if I left the tickets there." Bobby replied "No probs, Dad." Half an hour later Bobby returned to his dad who was patiently waiting outside the football pitch. He said to his dad, "Yep, they're on the kitchen table where you left them."

Sam worked in an office in Lemington. One day he walked into his boss's office and said, "I'll be honest with you, I know the economy isn't great, but I have three companies after me, and I would like to respectfully ask for a pay rise."

After a few minutes of haggling, his manager finally agreed to a 5% rise, and Sam happily got up to leave.

"By the way", asked the boss as Sam got up, "Which three companies are after you?"

"The electric company, the water company and the phone company", Sam replied.

Jim was having a pint in the Old George one night when in walked Simon, a very brash man from Sunderland. Jim couldn't help overhearing Simon trying to encourage some people to bet that they couldn't drink 20 pints in 20 minutes. Despite a great deal of persuasion, Simon was still failing in his attempt to make some money. Then he looked at Jim and said "Well what about you then? Are you interested?" Jim quickly drank the rest of his pint and left the pub.

Half an hour later, Jim walked back into the pub and said to Simon "OK, I'll take that bet."

Simon was delighted at the thought of winning the bet. But his excitement soon faded when Jim drank down the 20 pints in 19 minutes. Handing over the money, Simon said "When you left here earlier, where did you go?" Jim looked at him and replied "I had to go to pub down the road to see if I could do it first."

A man was hitchhiking back to Walker at night when he was caught in the middle of a big storm.

It was growing darker and no cars seemed to be coming by. The rain was so heavy that the man could hardly see a few feet ahead of him

Suddenly, he saw a car slowly coming towards him and stopped. Desperate for shelter and without thinking about it, he jumped into the car and closed the door. But then he realised there was nobody behind the wheel and the engine wasn't on

The car started moving slowly. The man looked out and saw that the car was approaching a bend in the road. Terrified, he started to pray, begging for his life. Suddenly, just before the car hit the verge, a disembodied hand seemed to appear from nowhere through the car window and turn the wheel. The man stared in horror at the hand, though it didn't come near him.

Soon after, the man noticed the lights of a pub appear down the road. He found the strength to leap out of the car and ran towards it. Wet and out of breath, he rushed inside and started telling everybody about the horrible experience he had just had.

A silence fell on the people in the pub when they realised how scared the student was.

Suddenly, the door opened, and two other people walked in.

Like the Walker man, they were also soaked and out of breath. Looking around, and seeing the man standing shaking at the bar, one said to the other...

"Look mate ... there's the idiot that got in the car while we were pushing it!"

A vicar from Newburn was travelling home one evening and was greatly annoyed when a young man, much the worse for drink, came and sat next to him on the bus.

"Young man," the vicar, declared in a rather pompous tone, "Do you not realise you are on the road to perdition?"

"Oh, drat and botheration," replied the drunken man, "I could have sworn this bus went to Dene."

A Mackem was walking through the desert when he stumbled across an old lamp. He picked it up and rubbed it and a genie appeared before him.

"You have two wishes," said the genie "Use them wisely."

So the Mackem said "I want an everlasting pie!"

The genie gave him a pie. The Mackem took a great chunk out of it and then said "Mmm that's smashing. I'll have another one of these."

A teacher at a Newcastle School was having a little trouble getting her year 11 pupils to understand grammar, "These are what we call the pronouns", she explained, "And the way we use them with verbs; I am, you are, he/she is" she was added, to blank looks.

Trying a different approach, she said, "Susan, give me a sentence with the pronoun, 'I' in it."

Susan began, "I is..."

"No, no, no, no, no NO, NO!" shouted the teacher, "Never, 'I is', always, 'I am'... now try again." Susan looked puzzled and a little hurt, thought a while then began again more quietly, "I... am...the ninth letter of the alphabet."

A boy from Gosforth was getting ready to start his new school term. Because he was getting older and more independent, his father gave him £2 for him to catch the bus home. But instead of getting on the bus, the boy ran behind it all the way home. His father came home and the boy proudly said, "Dad, I saved you £2 today because I ran behind the bus instead of getting on!" The man stormed out of the room, shouting "You should have run behind a taxi and saved me 40 quid you little..."

A Mackem was going for a job interview in Newcastle city centre and on the way there, he asked a local man for directions:

"Excuse me pal could you possibly tell me the quickest way to Newcastle city centre?"

The man answered, "You driving or walking, lad?"

The Mackem replied, "Driving."

The Geordie man nodded, saying "Yup, definitely the quickest way"

Johnny was down on his luck so he thought he would try getting a few odd jobs by calling at the big houses in Darrass Hall. After a few rejections, a man in one of the big houses thought he would give him a chance so he said "The porch needs painting so I'll give you £50 to paint it for me."

"That's great. You're a life saver. I'll get started straight away!" said the man

His one-off employer handed him a paintbrush and a tin of cream paint.

Time passed and the man came back, knocked on the door and said "There you go. It's all done! Painting completed and finished."

"Great. Here's your £50"

"Thanks very much. Oh by the way, it's a Ferrari, not a Porsche!"

Three friends, one from Newcastle University, one from Sunderland University and one from Manchester University, were out having a good time together at a funfair. They were just about to go on the helter-skelter when an old woman stepped in front of them.

"This is a magic ride," she said. "You will land in whatever you shout out on the way down."

"I'm up for this," said the Newcastle student and slid down the helter-skelter shouting "GOLD!" at the top of his voice. Sure enough, when he hit the bottom he found himself surrounded by thousands of pounds worth of gold coins.

The Manchester student went next and shouted "SILVER!" at the top of his voice. At the bottom he landed in more silver coinage than he could ever carry.

The Sunderland student went last and, launching himself from the top of the slide shouted "WEEEEEEE!"

A man from Walkerdene phoned his son in London three days before Christmas and said, "I hate to ruin your day, but I have to tell you that your mother and I are divorcing; forty-five years of misery is enough."

"Dad, what are you talking about?" his son shouted.

"We can't stand the sight of each other any longer" his father said, 'We're sick of each other and I'm sick of talking about this, so you call your sister in Manchester and tell her."

Frantic, the son called his sister, who yelled "Like hell they're getting divorced!" she shouted, "I'll take care of this!"

She immediately called her father and yelled at him "You are not getting divorced. Don't do a single thing until I get there.

I'm calling my brother back, and we'll both be there tomorrow. Until then, don't do a thing, DO YOU HEAR ME?". Then she hung up.

The old man hung up his phone and turned to his wife. "Done! They're coming for Christmas - and they're paying their own way."

A man was sat in a cafe in West Denton, he was fed up and had come out to cheer himself up and for a bit of company. He picked up the menu and noticed that it only featured three dishes: meatloaf, shepherd's pie and Pan Haggerty. The waitress came over to take his order. "I'll have the Pan Haggerty," said the man glumly, "and if you could throw in a few kind words that would be very welcome." The waitress left and returned a few minutes later with a plate of Pan Haggerty. She banged the plate on the table in front of the man and started to walk off. "Hey," said the man. "I got my dinner; how about those kind words?" The waitress turned, paused and said, "Don't eat the Pan Haggerty."